FEARSOME, SCARY, AND CREEPY ANIMALS

Sinister Snakes

Elaine Landau

Enslow Publishers, Inc.

40 Industrial Road PO Box 38
Box 398 Aldershot
Berkeley Heights, NJ 07922 Hants GU12 6BP
USA UK

http://www.enslow.com

For Sarah Sutin

Library of Congress Cataloging-in-Publication Data

Landau, Elaine.
    Sinister snakes / Elaine Landau.
        p. cm. — (Fearsome, scary, and creepy animals)
    Summary: Introduces snakers and why they sometimes attack humans, and
tells of some real-life snake attacks.
    Includes bibliographical references (p.   ).
    ISBN 0-7660-2057-6 (hardcover : alk. paper)
    1. Snakes—Juvenile literature. 2. Poisonous snakes—Juvenile literature.
3. Snakebites—Juvenile literature. [1. Snakes. 2. Poisonous snakes. 3. Snakebites.] I. Title.
QL666.O6 L323 2003
597.96'165--dc21   2002006939

Printed in the United States of America

10 9 8 7 6 5 4 3 2 1

To Our Readers: We have done our best to make sure all Internet addresses in this book were active and appropriate
when we went to press. However, the author and the publisher have no control over and assume no liability for the
material available on those Internet sites or on other Web sites they may link to. Any comments or suggestions can
be sent by e-mail to comments@enslow.com comments@enslow.com or to the address on the back cover.

Illustration Credits: © 1999 Artville, LLC., pp. 30 (map), 31 (both maps), 32 (both maps); © Corel Corporation, pp. 5, 8
(top), 13 (bottom), 17 (bottom), 23, 25, 26, 27 (both), 30 (inset), 31 (top inset), 34 (top); © Digital Vision/Picture Quest, pp.
5 (background), 6, 19; © Gary McVicker/Index Stock Imagery/PictureQuest, p. 39; Amy E. Conn/Associated Press, p. 7
(bottom); Associated Press, p. 11 (bottom); BCC, p. 32 (bottom inset); Frans Lemmens/Getty Images, p. 35 (top); George
Andrejko/Associated Press, p. 40; Getty Images, pp. 28, 38 (both); Hemera Technologies, Inc., pp. ii, iii, 7 (top), 8 (bottom),
10, 13 (top), 14 (top), 18 (top), 22 (both), 24, 33 (both), 34 (bottom); Jim Cole/Associated Press, p. 15; John Bavaro, p. 4;
LM Otero/Associated Press, p. 16; Mike Wintroath/Associated Press, p. 21; Pete
Carmichael/Getty Images, pp. i , 32 (top inset); Photo Researchers, Inc., p. 20; Ric
Frearson/Associated Press, p. 36; Richard Silverberg, p. 12; Science Photo Library, pp.
10 (background), 11 (top); Stephen Cooper/Getty Images, p. 35 (bottom); Stevain
Morgain/Associated Press, p. 18 (bottom); Tim Johnson/Associated Press, pp. 17
(top), 31 (bottom inset); Volker Steger/Science Photo Library, pp. 14 (bottom), 29.
Unless otherwise noted, borders and backgrounds © Corel Corporation, Inc.

Cover Illustration: © Gary McVicker/Index Stock Imagery/PictureQuest

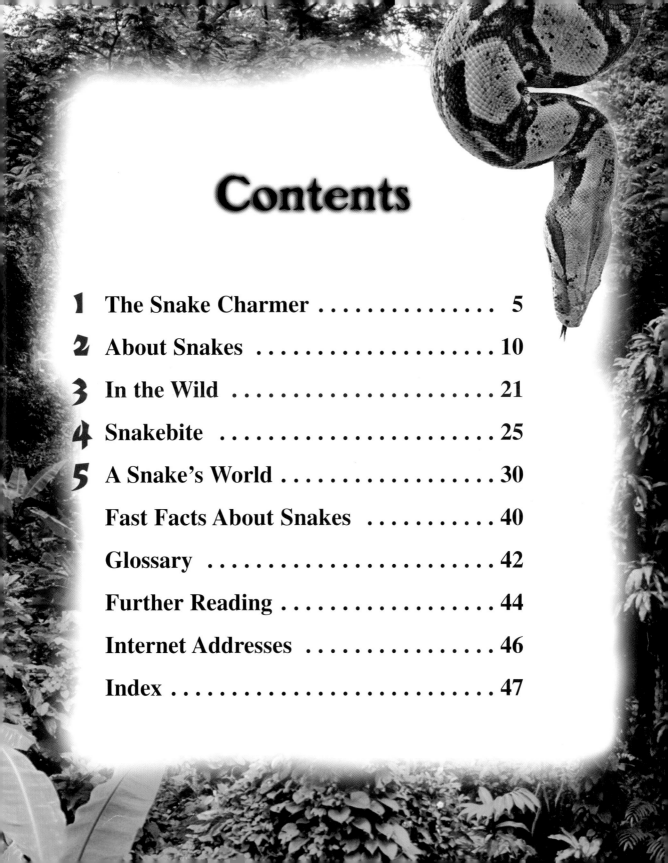

Contents

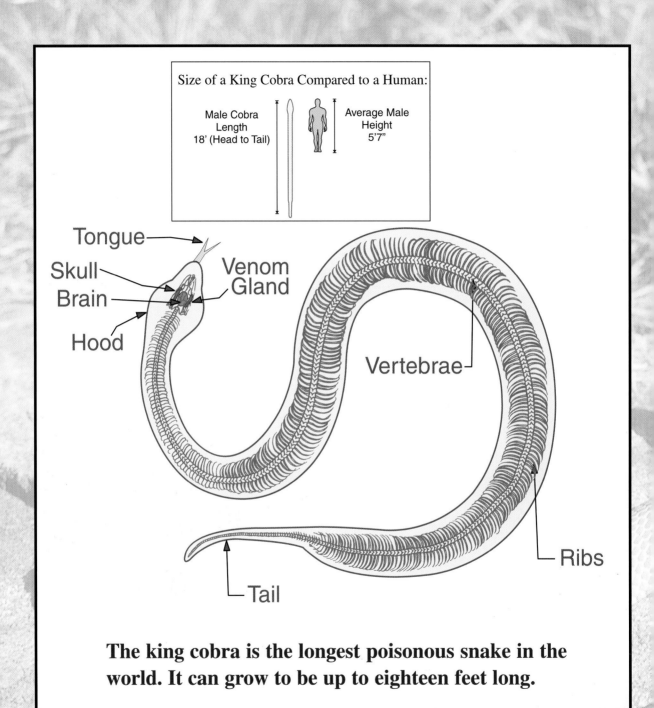

Size of a King Cobra Compared to a Human:

Male Cobra Length 18' (Head to Tail)

Average Male Height 5'7"

Tongue

Skull

Brain

Hood

Venom Gland

Vertebrae

Ribs

Tail

The king cobra is the longest poisonous snake in the world. It can grow to be up to eighteen feet long.

1. The Snake Charmer

It was an exciting day. A circus had come to Allentown, Pennsylvania. Nearly 500 people went to the show. The crowd liked the clowns. They clapped for the tightrope walker. They saw animal acts, too.

One animal act was extra special. It had a snake charmer. His name was John Walker. Walker performed with snakes. He had about ten snakes in his act. One was poisonous. That was the cobra. A cobra's bite is deadly. It can kill a person.

The cobra had been in a basket. Walker took it out. He set it down on a

Snake charmers often perform with dangerous and poisonous snakes. The snakes shown here are cobras.

table. The cobra raised the front of its body. Its head swayed back and forth. The audience thought the cobra was in a trance, but it was not. Snake charmers just want you to think that. Cobras lift their bodies for a different reason—they are on guard.

Less than a minute later, it happened. The snake suddenly leaned forward. It bit Walker. Some thought it was part of the act. They were wrong. Walker put the snake back in the basket. Then he said, "I've been bitten. Call 911."

Walker waited for the ambulance to come. His eyes were already watery and bloodshot. But he still made a call on his cell phone. He told the person on the other end, "I've been bitten by a cobra…. Just pray for me."

The snake

Cobras lift their bodies when they are on guard.

charmer was taken to Lehigh Valley Hospital. He was listed as a Class 1 patient. These are patients with life-threatening wounds. Walker was given antivenin serum. This medicine fights against the cobra's poison. Luckily, the hospital had some on hand. Walker survived. It was not his first snakebite. It might not be his last. Performing with poisonous snakes can be dangerous work.

Most people have seen live snakes. Everyone has seen pictures of them. Snakes are long, legless animals. They have been on Earth for a long time. There were even snakes 100 million years ago.

Snakes are cold-blooded. That does not mean they are

Antivenin serum fights the snake's poison in the body.

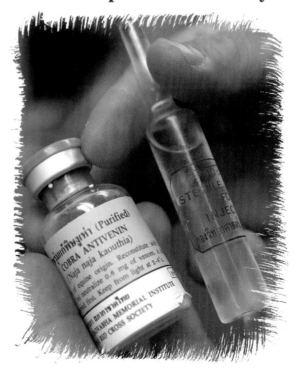

heartless killers. It has to do with their body temperature. A snake's body temperature changes with its surroundings.

Lying in the sun, its body temperature rises. In a cooler spot, a snake's body temperature goes down.

Snakes are reptiles. All reptiles are cold-blooded. Some crawl on the ground. Others creep on short legs.

Snakes stay warm by lying in the sun.

Snakes slide on their bellies. Lizards, turtles, and crocodiles are reptiles, too. They have short legs.

There are many different kinds of snakes. About 2,700 species, or kinds, live around the world. Not all snakes are poisonous. In fact, only about 15 percent of snakes are. Of these, about twenty-five types have caused human deaths. This book is about poisonous snakes. It takes a close look at a few snakes: snakes whose bites should be feared—snakes that should always be left alone.

Did you know...

Snakes do not have eyelids. They do not blink when they look at their prey. This may be where the story that snakes hypnotize their prey comes from. Snakes cannot actually hypnotize anything.

2. About Snakes

Do you think there is not much to know about snakes? Think again. Snakes are fascinating creatures. Here are some basic facts:

Body Shape

Some snakes are long and thick. Others are short and thin. Still others have flat sides. A snake may look like a leathery tube. However, all snakes have bones. Snakes are vertebrates. That means they have backbones.

Scales

Snakes may seem slimy, but they are not. They are covered with dry scales. Snakeskin has two layers. At times, the snake sheds (loses) its outer layer. This happens as a snake grows, or when the scales become worn. This process of skin-shedding is called molting.

Snakeskin can be different colors. Some snakes have brown or green skin to blend in with their surroundings. Other snakes are brightly colored. Many have interesting patterns and designs.

The colors of a snake's skin help it to blend in with its surroundings. The scales protect the snake and help it to move.

Senses

A snake has two eyes, one on each side of its head. But these reptiles do not have eyelids. Instead, clear scales cover their eyes. So their eyes always look open, even when they sleep.

A snake's eyes always look open, even when the snake is asleep.

11

A snake's ears cannot be seen. Snakes have inner ears that provide limited hearing.

Snakes have quite good eyesight, but they depend more on their sense of smell. A snake has a special organ for this. It is called Jacobson's organ. This organ is made up of two sacs in the snake's mouth. These sacs have many nerve endings. The nerve endings can detect (sense) odors.

The Jacobson's organ works with the snake's

When a snake flicks out its tongue, it picks up scent particles. The snake then pulls in its tongue, and the particles are transferred to the Jacobson's organ to detect odors.

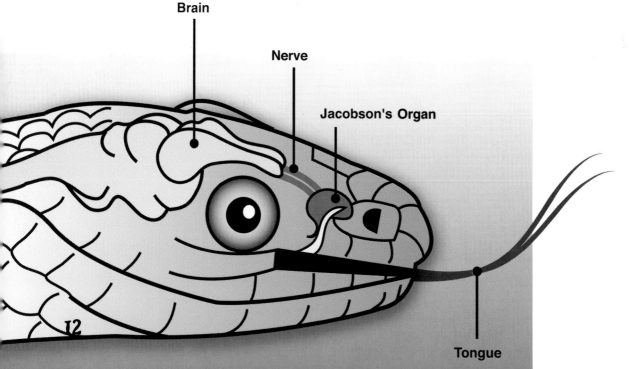

Brain

Nerve

Jacobson's Organ

Tongue

tongue. The snake sticks out its tongue. It picks up scents around it. Then the snake pulls its tongue back. The scents are brought to the Jacobson's organ. The Jacobson's organ helps the snake follow a scent trail. This is important in hunting prey. Prey are the animals snakes hunt as food.

Digestive System

Snakes do not chew their food. They swallow it whole. That means they eat their prey's entire body—even the bones. The only parts not digested are hair or feathers. Snakes are built to eat bulky food. Their stomachs widen to do so. Their stomachs also produce enzymes. These are substances that help break down the food.

Snakes swallow their food whole. Shown here is a corn snake eating a mouse.

Fangs and Venom

Some snakes poison their prey. They use their fangs for this. Fangs are long, pointed teeth. They are in the snake's upper jaw. The snake bites its prey with its fangs. Poison is sent through the fangs. This poison is known as venom. The venom kills the snake's victim.

There are two large groups of poisonous snakes. One group is known as vipers. Vipers have long front fangs. When a viper strikes, its fangs come out. Other times, the fangs are folded back inside the roof of the snake's mouth. Elapids are the other type of poisonous snake. Elapids have short fangs, but their fangs are not moveable.

Snakes poison their prey with venom that is sent through the fangs.

14

Vipers include such snakes as the rattlesnake, cottonmouth, and copperhead. Among the elapids are the cobra and the black mamba. Here is a closer look at these poisonous snakes:

Rattlesnakes

There are about 30 different types of rattlesnakes. These snakes have triangle-shaped heads. Their heads are broader than their necks. Rattlesnakes have a rattle at the end of their tails. Their rattles are made of pieces of

Rattlesnakes rattle their tails as a warning to stay away.

This is a diamondback rattlesnake. Its skin has a diamond-shaped pattern.

a horn-like material. They are loosely joined together. Rattlesnakes rattle their tails when they are threatened (afraid). It is a warning to stay away.

Rattlesnakes are pit vipers. Pit vipers have two openings or pits beneath their nostrils. These pits sense heat. Pit vipers sense the heat given off by their prey's body. They can even find prey in the dark.

Not all rattlesnakes look the same. Some rattlesnakes have diamond-shaped patterns on their skin. Others have speckles or stripes. Their colors are different, too.

Copperheads

Like the rattlesnake, the copperhead is a pit viper. This snake is quite colorful. Most of its body is pinkish-

brown. It has darker, chestnut-colored bands on its back and sides. Its head is coppery red, which is why it is called a copperhead. Copperheads are between two and three feet long.

Copperhead snakes get their name from the copper coloring on their heads.

Cottonmouths (Also Known as Water Moccasins)

Like rattlesnakes and copperheads, the cottonmouth is a pit viper. Adult cottonmouths are about three and a half feet long. When fully grown, these snakes are

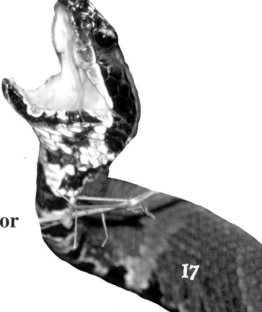

Cottonmouth snakes have whitish (or cotton-colored) mouths.

brownish-black. The inner lining of this snake's mouth is white. That is why it is called a cottonmouth.

Cobras

Cobras are a group of poisonous snakes. They are sometimes called hooded snakes. They do not really have a hood, but they can move their ribs to flatten their necks. This looks like a hood. Some fully grown cobras are very big. A king cobra is the largest. It can grow to be up to eighteen feet long. Cobras differ in color. Some can be yellowish.

King cobras are the largest cobras. The one shown here is not fully grown, but may grow to be up to eighteen feet long.

Others are a darker brown. Fully-grown king cobras may be yellow, green, brown, or black. Their throats are light yellow or cream-colored.

Cobras strike in two ways. Some bite their victims. The poison from their fangs enters their prey's body. Other cobras squirt their poison. They tilt back their head, then squirt the poison into their victim's eyes.

Some snakes attack by spitting venom into the eyes of their prey.

Black Mambas

Black mambas are large, deadly snakes. They are usually between six and eight feet long, but some have grown to fourteen feet in length. Black Mambas have coffin-shaped heads. They are slender snakes that look like whips.

The black mamba moves quickly. In a short burst of speed, it can go fifteen miles per hour. There are many tales about how mambas outran humans to bite them. The black mamba has been called the fastest snake on Earth.

The black mamba's venom is extremely powerful. Just two drops can kill a human. Some people have died within twenty minutes of being bitten. The black mamba is not really black. It is brownish gray. Its name comes from the inside of its mouth, which is purplish-black in color.

Black mambas look like whips, with coffin-shaped heads.

3. In the Wild

Picture a forest, one filled with many kinds of animals. Among these are rattlesnakes. A large rattlesnake is on the prowl. It is looking for a meal. But it needs to find a good hiding place first—a spot where it can wait for its prey.

The rattlesnake moves slowly through the forest. It picks up a scent (smell). It is coming from a well-traveled path. Mice use this path. Their scent is still fresh. The rattlesnake's prey will soon be back. The snake waits quietly near a fallen log. It is hidden in the brush.

Soon, the rattlesnake senses something. A mouse is close by. The snake waits until the

A rattlesnake will wait until its prey approaches, then strike out with its fangs.

Rattlesnakes typically eat small animals like mice, but sometimes humans can be bitten, as well.

mouse approaches. Then, it strikes. Its mouth closes around the prey. The snake's fangs give out its venom. The poison flows into the trapped mouse. Seconds later, the rattlesnake releases its victim. The mouse tries to run, but it does not get very far. The poison slows it down. Before long, the mouse dies.

The rattlesnake flicks its tongue several times. This helps it to again pick up the mouse's scent. It finds the mouse easily. The rattlesnake swallows the dead animal whole. It eats the mouse headfirst.

That is how a rattlesnake hunts in the wild. Humans are not rattlesnake prey, or food for any other snake. Yet at times, people are bitten. This almost happened to some children in Georgia. They were spared, however, thanks to Dixie, the children's pet pit bull terrier.

Frank Humphries, a nine-year-old boy, was one of the youngsters. He and his seven-year-old twin sisters were

A pit bull terrier, like the one shown here, saved Frank Humphries and his sisters.

outdoors. They came across a cottonmouth. This snake can be quick to strike. Its venom is extremely deadly, as well.

But it was Dixie to the rescue! The dog grabbed the snake in its mouth. Dixie shook the cottonmouth until it was dead.

The children were not harmed, but their brave dog was. The snake had bitten Dixie twice on the face. The dog was rushed to the animal hospital where it was given antivenin. Dixie lived. The Georgia Animal Hall of Fame later honored the pet.

Did you know...

Sometimes, adult male snakes fight each other. They lift their bodies and wrap themselves together, trying to push each other down. The battle ends when one snake gives up and slithers away.

4. Snakebite

Where would you find snakes? Most people would say outdoors. You might see a snake in the forest, along a mountain trail, or even in the desert. But that is not always the case.

Seven-year-old Jonathan Bruce found a snake in his house in Ohio. No one saw the snake enter. But sometimes, snakes crawl into homes and barns. They may be looking for a warm place in the winter or a cool, shady spot in the summer.

A copperhead was in Jonathan's bedroom. It

A copperhead snake, like the one shown here, was hiding in Jonathan Bruce's room.

Snakes are commonly found in the forest. . .

was probably looking for mice. Copperheads mostly eat mice. The snake was lying beneath the boy's bed. Jonathan reached for a toy there. That was when the copperhead bit him.

Jonathan's father killed the snake. The boy was taken to the hospital by helicopter. He was treated there for the bite. Jonathan made a good recovery.

Jonathan had been surprised to find a snake in his

. . .or in the desert.

room. Things were different for twenty-year-old Teddy Tarrant. A snake also bit him. But it was his pet cobra.

Tarrant had been trying to pose the snake for a picture. The snake had other ideas. It bit Tarrant on the thumb.

The young man was taken to a nearby hospital. However,

27

there was a problem. The medical center did not have the antivenin he needed. Neither did other hospitals in the area.

Tarrant had to be flown out of state. He was brought to Miami, Florida. That is where Venom 1 is. Venom 1 is a special rescue unit. It is set up to help poisonous snakebite victims. Venom 1 has the nation's largest supply of antivenin. It carries sixteen different types of antivenin, which covers 90 percent of the world's poisonous snakes. Members of this unit are specially trained. They are antivenin experts.

When he arrived in Miami, Tarrant was very ill. He was

It is important to remember that cobras are dangerous creatures, even if some people keep them for pets.

paralyzed (unable to move). He could not breathe on his own. A machine known as a ventilator kept him alive.

Tarrant was treated with antivenin. Luckily, it was not too late. He was able to go home a few days later. By then, he was on his way to recovery.

Every year, between 10,000 and 20,000 snakebites are reported. Usually, less than ten snakebites a year result in death.

Venom is milked from poisonous snakes and used to make antivenin serum and pain-killing medications.

5. A Snake's World

People often think of poisonous snakes as a group. But there are many differences among them. Scientists have studied poisonous snakes. Here is some of what they know:

Habitat (Where Poisonous Snakes Live)

Rattlesnakes

Rattlesnakes are found from lower Canada to South America. Many live in the United States. They are often seen in the southwestern desert areas.

Cottonmouths

Cottonmouths, or water moccasins, are found in the southeastern United States. These snakes live in watery places. They may be spotted in swamps or around lakes and rivers.

Copperheads

Copperheads live in the United States. They are mostly found in the east. However, these snakes also live in Nebraska, Texas, and other western areas. Copperheads like places with vines and plants.

Cobras

Cobras are found in the East Indies, Africa, and southern Asia.

Black Mambas

Black mambas live in southern Africa. They prefer low, open areas. These snakes are often spotted near open wooded spots and rocky places.

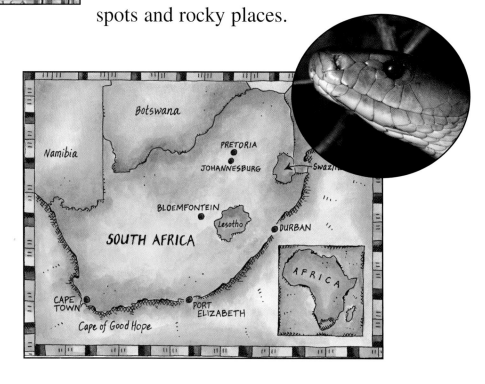

Diet (What They Eat)

Rattlesnakes

Most rattlesnakes eat birds and mice, but they also hunt other prey. The larger rattlesnakes eat squirrels, chipmunks, prairie dogs, and rabbits. Smaller rattlesnakes often eat lizards and other small snakes. Rattlesnakes in damp areas eat frogs and fish, as well.

Cottonmouths

These snakes feed on small snakes, mice, frogs, and other small animals. They also sometimes eat insects.

Cobras

Cobras eat many types of small animals. These can include birds, rats, mice, frogs, and fish.

Black Mambas

Black mambas feed on rats, mice, squirrels, birds, and many other small animals.

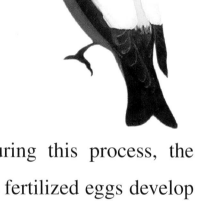

Reproduction (How Young Snakes Are Born)

Snakes mate to reproduce. During this process, the female's eggs are fertilized. The fertilized eggs develop into new snakes.

Most female snakes lay their eggs in tree stumps, logs, or other places. The female king cobra builds a nest of leaves and branches. It lays from twenty to fifty eggs there. The female remains on top of the nest. She guards the eggs. The male stays close by, as well.

Cobras lay their eggs in tree stumps and logs.

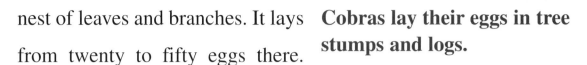

The young snakes grow inside the eggs. At the right time, they hatch. The newborn snakes are on their own. They must find food or die.

Rattlesnakes do not look after their young.

Some snakes do not lay eggs. Instead, they give birth to live young. Among these are rattlesnakes, cottonmouths, and copperheads. But these snakes do not look after their young, either.

Tips to Avoid Snakebites

People live throughout most of the world. Poisonous snakes do, too. There is room for both, but people need to know how to behave around snakes.

Many snakebites can be avoided. But people need to know what to do if they are bitten. The following tips may be helpful:

Many snake bites can be avoided if you remember a few tips.

❖ Never keep a poisonous snake as a pet. These are wild animals. They do not make good pets.

❖ Use caution around any poisonous snakes your friends or neighbors have. Never try to play with a poisonous snake.

❖ If you see a poisonous snake outdoors, leave it alone. Do not try to catch it. Do not try to kill it. If the snake is near a home or playground, tell a responsible adult.

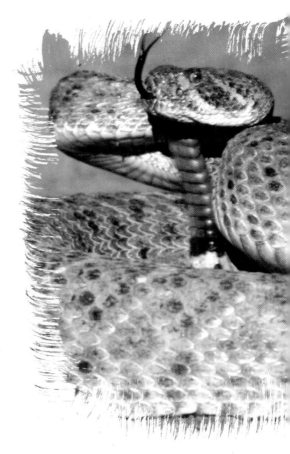

What if Someone Is Bitten?

❖ Try to stay calm.

❖ Call a responsible adult.

❖ Get to a hospital emergency room quickly.

❖ Remain as still as possible while waiting to see a doctor. Movement spreads the venom.

❖ Keep the bitten area below the heart.

Many poisonous snakes are wild and beautiful. Some kill harmful pests that destroy farm crops. Snakes are also helpful in controlling rodents (mice and rats). Poisonous snakes have their place in nature. We need to treat them with respect and keep our distance.

Fast Facts About SNAKES

❖ A rattlesnake does not always rattle its tail before biting.

❖ There are no snakes in frozen regions. They cannot survive there. Interestingly, there are also no snakes in Ireland or New Zealand.

❖ Some people eat snakes. This is not uncommon in Hong Kong. A number of restaurants there keep cages of live snakes. Customers pick out the ones they want. The snakes are killed and cooked for them.

❖ Humans have found uses for snakeskin. It has been used to make belts, shoes, purses, and other items. As a result, some snakes are at risk of dying out.

❖ In the United States, poisonous snakes are part of some religious services. These groups bring the snakes to prayer meetings in boxes. Church members put their hands in the boxes. They pull out the snakes. They are not afraid. They believe that their faith will protect them. Sadly, some people have died doing this.

❖ A single bite from a king cobra can kill a large elephant. These is also also enough venom in one bit to kill ten to thirteen humans.

❖ More than half the snakebites in the United States involve children.

❖ Scientists are studying the black mamba's venom. Someday, it may be used as a painkiller.

❖ Antivenin is very costly. A small amount costs between $55 and $1,200.

Glossary

antivenin serum	Medicine to combat the poison from snakebites.
bloodshot	A condition in which a person's eyes are red and irritated.
cold-blooded	A body temperature that changes with its surroundings.
detect	Sense.
elapids	Snakes with short front fangs. These fangs do not move.
enzymes	Substances that help break down food.
fangs	Long, pointed teeth.
habitat	Surroundings or environment.
hypnotize	To daze or put in a trance.

Jacobson's organ	A special organ in a snake's brain that helps it pick up scents.
molting	The loss of the outer layer of a snake's skin.
paralyze	Unable to move.
pit vipers	Snakes that have two openings or pits beneath their nostrils.
prey	Animals that are hunted for food.
scent	Smell or odor.
sheds	Loses.
species	A particular type or kind.
threatened	Afraid.
venom	A snake's poison.
Venom 1	A special snakebite rescue unit.
ventilator	A machine that helps people breathe.
vipers	Snakes that have long, moveable front fangs.

Further Reading

Burns, Diane L. *Snakes, Salamanders, and Lizards*. Minnetonka, Minn.: Northword Press, 1998.

Demuth, Patricia. *Snakes*. New York: Grosset & Dunlap, 1993.

George, Linda. *Cobras*. Minnetonka, Minn.: Capstone Press, 1998.

Gerholdt, James E. *King of Cobras*. Minneapolis, MN: Abdo & Daughters, 1996.

Linley, Mike. *Snakes*. New York: Thomson Learning, 1993.

Markle, Sandra. *Outside and Inside Snakes*. New York: Atheneum, 1998.

Robson, Denny. *Snakes*. New York: Gloucester Press, 1992.

Schnieper, Claudia. *Snakes: Silent Hunters.* Minneapolis, MN: Carolrhoda, 1995.

Simon, Seymour. *Snakes.* New York: Harper Collins, 1992.

Stoops, Erik D. and Annette T. Wright. *Snakes.* New York: Sterling Publishing, 1992.

Internet Addresses

American International Rattlesnake Museum

This museum has the largest collection of live rattlesnakes in the world. The Web site has great pictures and fun facts.

<http://www.rattlesnakes.com>

National Geographic's King Cobra Site

This Web site contains lots of information on the world's largest poisonous snake.

<http://www.nationalgeographic.com/kingcobra/ index-n.html>

Index